CONVERSATIONS IN CLAVE

The Ultimate Technical Study of Four-Way Independence in Afro-Cuban Rhythms

- Fundamental concepts of the clave and Afro-Cuban rhythms
- Dexterity, independence and four-way coordination exercises
- Developing improvisational ideas
- Stylistic groove transcriptions: Cascara, Guaguanco, Mambo, Macuta, Songo, Mozambique

Transcriptions and Annotations by Ken Ross

by Horacio Hernandez
"El Negro"

"El Negro" at Carriage House Studios, Stamford, CT.

Conversations In Clave
By Horacio "El Negro" Hernandez

■ Project Coordinator
Ray Brych

■ Cover Design
Debbie Lipton

■ Cover Photo
Neil Zlozower

■ Book Design and Layout, Music Typesetting
Dancing Planet MediaWorks™

■ Audio Recording, Mixing, and Mastering
Dancing Planet MediaWorks™, Cresskill, NJ

Dedication

I would like to dedicate this book to the three men of my home: Abuelo Horacio, Papa Horacito and my brother Tavito. Through these three men I received all the music.

To my mother Josefina, who always fed me with love and had the patience to put up with me playing drums all day.

To Jennifer and Claudia, who truly are my two jewels.

To my love Margaret Sterlacci (my better half).

Acknowledgements

Horacio would like to extend his sincere gratitude and appreciation to the following people:

To Ken Ross and Stefano DiRubbo for their help in creating this book.

Giancarlo Toffanelli, Roberto Evangelisti, Paulo LaRosa, Santiago Rieter, Damaris Favier, Roberto Vizcaino, Pancho Quinto, Paquito D'Rivera, Nicolas Reinoso, Gonzalo Rubalcaba, Chucho Valdes, Marilu Menendez, Ileana Padron, Raul Artilles, Tito and Margie Puente, Peter Erskine, Giovanni Hidalgo, Robbie Ameen, Ken Ross, Michael Sterlacci, Johnny and Jill Almendras, Scott Miller, Steve Ettleson, John King, John DeChristopher, Colin Scofield, Armand Zildjian, Craigie Zildjian, Lenny DiMuzio, Remo Belli, Carol and Joe Calato, Richie Goad, Derek Wiseman, Mike Farriss, Terry West, Andy Ito, Ryan Smith, Neil Graham, John Vandermullen, Claudio Galinski.

Manolo Badrena, Larry Clothier, Larry Baeder Charlie Torres, Diane Lotny, Stu Deutsch, Pam Gore, Bill Saragosa, Ron and Isabel Spagnardi, Rick Van Horn, Bill Miller, Mauro Salvatori and Fabrizio at Quemme, Tulio Granatello, Walfredo and Debbie Reyes, Carl Perazzo, Raul Rekow, Andy and Jerry Gonzalez, Papo and Lena Vazquez, Jason O'Laine, Felix Villaplana and the Summer Sunday Rumba at Central Park, Kip Hanrahan, Gladys Llanes, Carmen Perez, Steve Houghton, Becky, Carlitos Del Puerto, Dean Anderson, Berklee College of Music, Percussive Arts Society, Paul Frederick, Ralph Angelillo, Darren Abraham, David Ortega, Michel and Sandra Camilo, and especially Pearl Drums, Zildjian Cymbals, Evans Drumheads, Regal Tip Drumsticks, Shure Microphones, and Protector Cases.

Tito Puente and Horacio warming up before a gig

To Tito:
Your warmth and generosity and guidance will live forever in my heart.

Negro

September 29, 2000

About the Author

Grammy Award winner and internationally renowned recording artist Horacio "El Negro" Hernandez was born in Havana, Cuba, into a family with rich musical heritage, deeply rooted in traditional Cuban music and well-versed in American jazz currents. His own talent became evident early. At age twelve, "El Negro" was accepted by the prestigious Escuela Nacional de Arte, where he majored in drums and percussion. There he studied with the finest Cuban teachers, including Fausto Garcia Rivera, himself a student of famed American teachers Lawrence Stone and Henry Adler, and Enrique Pla, the drummer for the ground-breaking group "Irakere," and Santiago Rieter, the most influential of modern Cuban drummer-percussionists.

While still very young, Horacio began to work professionally in the group of well known Cuban saxophonist Nicolas Reynoso. As part of the exciting musical scene of 1980s Havana, he worked with all its dominant musicians; among them Paquito D'Rivera, Lucia Huergo, Arturo Sandoval, and German Velazco. He quickly became the most in-demand drummer of Egrem, the major recording studios in Cuba and making hundreds of recordings with them.

In 1980, "Negro" joined Cuban pianist and composer Gonzalo Rubalcaba's innovative group, "Proyecto." He played, toured and recorded with the group for ten years. Though he continued to work and record with the best Cuban and international musicians, including Dizzy Gillespie's United Nations Orchestra, it was with Rubalcaba that he developed his distinct drumming style—the potent mixture of Afro-Cuban and jazz elements that has made him an artist of extraordinary power and musical versatility.

He moved to Rome in 1990 and soon became the energizing force in that city's jazz and Latin music circles, working and recording with Pino Danielle, Gary Bartz, Steve Turre, Gary Smulyan and Mike Stern. He also formed his own band Tercer Mundo. During his stay in Rome he chaired the Latin Percussion department of the Centro di Percussione Timba and taught at the Universita della Musica, while also conducting many drum clinics throughout Italy.

Hernandez arrived in New York in 1993 and immediately began to work with such celebrated jazz musicians as Paquito D'Rivera, Dave Valentin, Jerry Gonzalez and the Fort Apache Band, the Ed Simon Trio, Anthony Jackson, Kip Hanrahan, David Sanchez, Papo Vazquez, Steve Turre and the Sanctified Shells, Santi Debriano and the Panamaniacs, the Cepeda family's Afro-Rican Jazz, Giovanni Hidalgo, Arturo Sandoval, Regina Carter, Chico O'Farrill and Tito Puente, as well as with In the Spirit, a rhythm and blues/rock/funk band.

"El Negro" was also a member of the Michel Camilo Trio, playing percussion on Camilo's original soundtrack for the film *Two Much*. He was the featured drummer for San Francisco's memorable concert, *Irakere West*, lead by famed Cuban pianist, Chucho Valdes, with special guest star Carlos Santana. He has become a member of the Tropi-Jazz All-Stars

under the direction of Tito Puente, a band that includes Hilton Ruiz, Eddie Palmieri, Giovanni Hidalgo, Dave Valentin, Juan Pablo Torres and Charlie Sepulveda among other Latin greats.

After several international engagements as a guest artist with Roy Hargrove's Crisoul band, (the band features Hargrove, Gary Bartz, Frank Lacey, David Sanchez, Changuito, Jon Benitez, Anga Diaz, Russel Malone and Chucho Valdes), Hernandez joined the band to record their first CD entitled *Habana*. This debut recording earned Crisoul the 1997 Grammy Award for best recording in the Latin-jazz category.

Horacio also recorded with Michel Camilo, John Patitucci and Anthony Jackson on a Camilo release entitled "Thru My Eyes." "El Negro's" true essence is captured on the track "A Night in Tunisia." He has also appeared with McCoy Tyner.

In 1997 Negro toured with Santana and recorded two tracks for Santana's Grammy Award-winning "Supernatural" recording.

He is a member of the faculty of the Drummer's Collective and the New School in New York and the Percussion Institute of Technology in Los Angeles, where he is teaching as part of the Master Artists series with Steve Houghton and Gary Chaffee. He also conducts regular workshops at the prestigious Berklee School of Music in Boston and the Stanford University Jazz Workshop in Palo Alto. Horacio is an endorser and clinician for Pearl Drums and Zildjian cymbals and has been a featured artist at numerous industry events, including NAMM and the Percussive Arts Society International Convention.

Preface

This book was born after experiencing the combination of a long career as a performing artist mixed with vital experiences as a teacher in different parts of the world. From the debut of my teaching I found a big wall: many of the books regarding Afro-Cuban styles were books about patterns only. Students were able to learn the correct patterns but then didn't know what to do with them. Some recent publications have remedied this shortcoming, but once students learned these patterns they developed no freedom to move within, or play fills, or do anything but play the patterns themselves. This is a long way from what playing Afro-Cuban music—or any music—really is.

When I first became interested in jazz, my teacher, Santiago Rieter, explained to me, "You must first work on independence and coordination, and only after that will you be able to work on the different styles inside of jazz. BUT FIRST GET THE COORDINATION!" It was with this advice that I began to study Jim Chapin's book (Four-Way Coordination) and only now do I understand that it was not only a method to develop freedom against the jazz ride cymbal pattern. It was also a great, great lesson on learning how to listen to different voices at the same time. In other words, how to be able to hear multiple rhythms from multiple sound sources at the same time. This is, in fact, the key to high level drum set and percussion performance.

In this book I continue to employ the same concepts as those of Jim Chapin, but here I apply it to the world of Afro-Cuban music. This book will assist you in gaining the coordination you will need to study and master the many different rhythms of the Afro-Cuban styles, and to feel free when playing them. As you become more familiar with these rhythms, these studies will also allow you to hear and create variations from the rhythmic foundations of the Afro-Cuban tradition.

I highly recommend getting very close to the whole Afro-Cuban percussion instrument family—tumbadora, bongos, paila, guiro, maracas, clave, campanas, bata, etc. It is pertinent to be able to recognize and eventually learn the distinct rhythms of each of these instruments. We can't forget that this style was created long before the 1920s when drumset was born, and therefore our style of playing contemporary drumset is derivative of the sound and language of the whole Afro-Cuban percussion section.

On a technical note: all of the exercises in this book are written using the rumba clave, but only because it is my musical preference. It is not better or more important than any of the other clave rhythms. In my view, it is more syncopated and creates more intricate and exact subdivisions so I feel more creative with it. Of course, you should use the son and 6/8 clave too.

The first and most important step is to understand the clave and the relation between eight-note and triplet rhythms that exist simultaneously in all Afro-Cuban music. We must also think about the MELODIC rhythms played by the various percussion instruments. The Afro-Cuban percussion section is comprised of this combination of clave, coexisting duple and triple rhythms and the melodic sonorities of each instrument. This book will help you develop a melodic hearing and phrasing as your rhythmic coordination grows.

Finally, and simultaneously with the study of this book, it is very important to LISTEN TO THE MUSIC YOU ARE ATTEMPTING TO LEARN. Listen to every type of Afro-Cuban music. Listen to the percussion section, but also focus on every musical instrument's part—piano, voice, bass, guitar, etc. You will see how everyone is playing their own rhythm along with their own melody.

Negro

June 1, 1999

Giovanni Hidalgo, "El Negro" and Jose Luis "Changuito" Quintana

Table of Contents

Part 6

Part 7

Part 8

Part 1

Fundamental Concepts of the Clave Rhythm

Horacio with the great Elvin Jones

The Clave Rhythm

The key to understanding Cuban music begins with the clave. The word, literally translated, means key. With this key we can learn how to phrase and interpret the music with authenticity and the correct feel.

The clave is a two-measure rhythm that serves as a reference point for all the rhythms, melodies, song-forms, and dances in Cuban music. This clave rhythm is always present in the music, even if it is not actually being played.

There are four basic clave patterns in Cuban music. The son clave, rumba clave, $\frac{6}{8}$ clave, and the Bembe clave. The two-measure pattern can either be 2:3 (meaning with two beats in the first measure and

three beats in the second measure), or 3:2 (meaning three beats in the first measure and two beats in the second measure).

Within the arrangement of a piece of music the direction of the clave may be either 3:2 or 2:3 in any given section. The exception is the Bembe clave. Once set in motion, the "direction" of the clave never changes.

It is important to understand and master these four clave patterns and their related concepts—how to hear, feel, and phrase them—before moving forward. This section lays the foundation for the remaining material in this book and your control of this material is essential.

Audio Note: On the recording the following examples are played on a woodblock. They can also be played on any sound source on your drum set—side of floor tom, rim of a drum, closed hihat, cymbal bell, cowbell and the like.

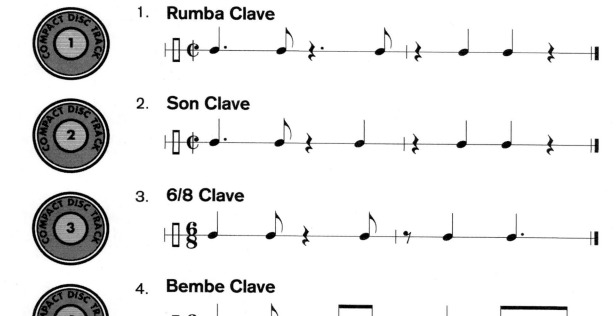

1. **Rumba Clave**

2. **Son Clave**

3. **6/8 Clave**

4. **Bembe Clave**

Rumba Clave

The rumba clave is unique in the fact that it can be phrased a number of ways, depending on the musical situation, of course. Sometimes this clave is played with a "strict four feel" and sometimes with a "six feel." Other times the phrasing falls somewhere between these two (duple and triple) meters. The standard notation system cannot do justice to this rhythm or "feel," as it is impossible to capture this feel in writing, and attempting to do so and then perform the written version would diminish the integrity of the music. However, the following examples can help you to visualize the clave rhythm and obtain a starting place for your studies of combining these two superimposed feels (meters). I suggest that you listen to a variety of Afro-Cuban music and feel how clave is phrased in each instance.

Practice playing the clave rhythm (right hand) on a wood block, or the side (shell) of the floor tom. Play the subdivisions quietly with the left hand on another sound source such as the hihat and listen carefully to the phrasing. Practice each two measure pattern until you feel comfortable with your rhythmic execution and your sound.

Audio Note: On the recording the following examples are played on a woodblock and the snare drum. They can be played on any two distinct sound sources on your set.

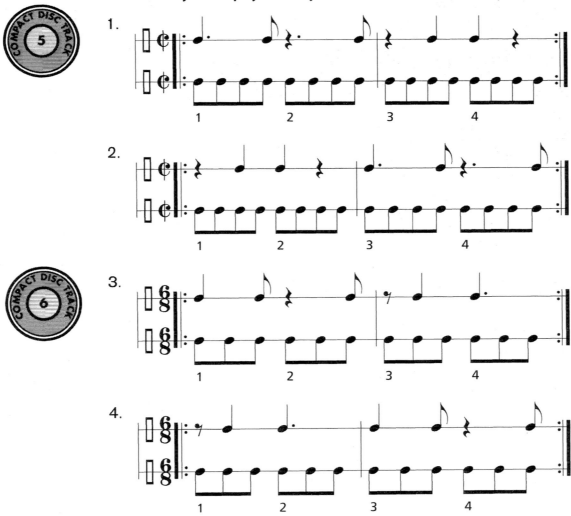

Combination Phrasing

Here we see the clave rhythm outlined in both 6/8 and cut-time. Notice that the notes with the "x" notehead outline the clave within the given subdivisions. As explained earlier, the 3-2 and 2-3 markings designate the direction of the clave.

Practice playing the x-notes with one hand while playing the subdivisions with the other hand. Listen carefully to the phrasing of the clave rhythm. The objective of these exercises is to develop and internalize a sense of phrasing that is relaxed, swinging, and authentic.

Afro-Cuban music can be played with a strict "four feel," a "six feel," or it can be phrased both ways, depending upon the musical situation. This is similar to jazz music. An example is the way a jazz ride pattern can be played as a strict dotted eight and sixteenth feel, or the more laid back triplet feel. Another example is the New Orleans shuffle, that falls somewhere between the two (duple and triple) feels— in the cracks.

Practice these exercises until you can comfortably "shift" between feels. It is essential, however, that you listen to recordings and performances of Afro-Cuban music to better understand the proper phrasing.

Note: the "x" notehead outlines the clave rhythm.

Audio Note: On the recording the following examples are played on the closed hihat and the snare drum. They can be played on any two distinct sound sources on your set.

Clave Phrasing: Rhythmic Analysis

These exercises are written in cut-time—$\frac{2}{2}$—a common meter in Afro-Cuban music. Notice how the $\frac{6}{8}$ feel translates to triplets in cut-time. Try playing Exercises 1 through 8 on two sound sources while tapping your foot in two pulses to the measure. If you play only the clave rhythm (the "x" noteheads), you will hear a certain "elasticity" in the rhythm.

Audio Note: On the recording the following examples are played on a woodblock and the snare drum. They can be played on any two distinct sound sources on your set.

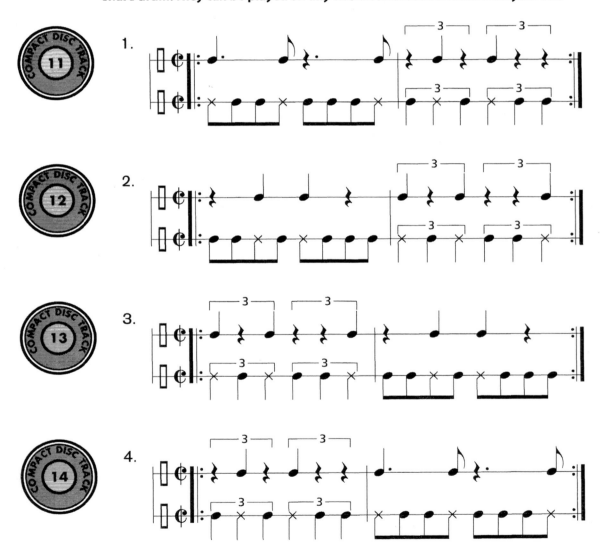

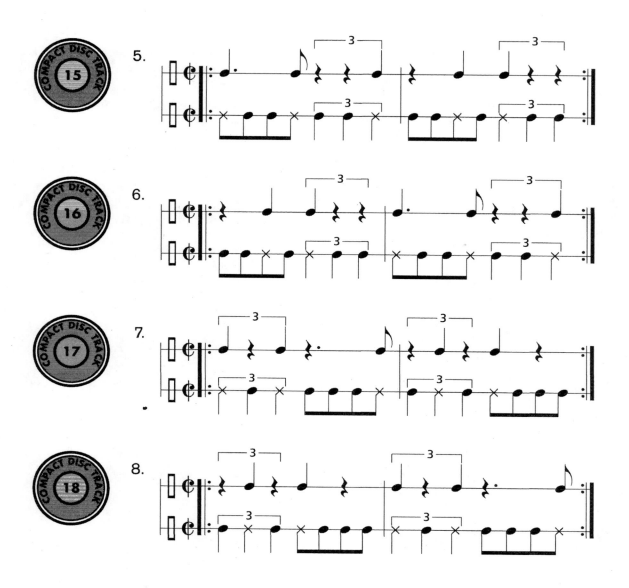

1

Clave Phrasing Exercises

The following exercises continue with the techniques and concepts presented in the last section. The notation in this section presents another way of looking at the rhythms, but the underlying elements—the elasticity of the feel and the superimposed duple and triple meter—remain the same. Practicing these exercises will help you get the correct phrasing of the clave rhythm while naturally incorporating this simultaneous duple-triple rhythmic combination.

Audio Note: In these examples the clave rhythm—"x" noteheads—is played on a woodblock, the standard notes on the snare drum and the left foot is playing the downbeats of each bar—the "1" of each bar—on the hihat.

1.

2.

3.

4.

5.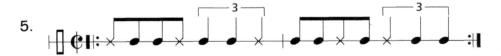

6.

7.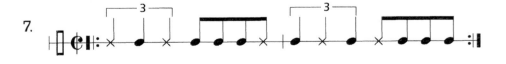

8.

Part 2

Achieving Dexterity With the Clave Rhythm

Horacio sitting in with Peter Erskine at the PASIC show in Anaheim, CA

Technical Exercises

Rhythmic Permutations With Rumba Clave

Following is a series of permutation exercises designed to develop your independence, coordination, and sense of phrasing in this style of music. The hihat rhythm, played with the foot, is an important reference point, because it marks the downbeat of each measure and helps you to lock in the time.

The clave rhythm is without a doubt the most important rhythm in all Afro-Cuban musical styles, for it serves as a reference point for all the rhythms and melodies, from the point of their composition right through to their arranging and performance.

The clave rhythm, played here with the right hand, can be played on any number of sound sources, such as a cowbell, woodblock (or L.P. Jamblock), auxiliary hihat, or the shell of the floor tom. Keep in mind the timbre and feeling you are trying to achieve. It should relate to the percussion instruments traditionally played in this style of music, especially if you wish to play with an authentic sound.

I also suggest that you practice Part 1 with your left hand playing clave and your right hand playing the variations. Don't be afraid to break-up the rhythms around the drumset once you feel comfortable with the exercises.

Finally, you can try going through these exercises with the 2-3 clave position. In other words, simply reverse the clave so that the measure with the two quarter notes is played first.

Note: The notation and suggested orchestration of each of the following exercises is provided at each rhythmic pattern.

2

Rumba Clave With One-Note Variations

The first ostinato system key consists of the clave in the right hand (or left hand if you are left-handed) with the hihat foot playing the downbeats (the first note) of each bar. Remember that you can play the clave pattern on any sound on your drum set/percussion setup (i.e., side of floor tom, rim of any drum, closed hihat, second hihat, bell of cymbal, cowbell, jam block). You can also play your hihat foot part on the hihat itself, or on a jam block or cowbell mounted on a foot-bracket for playing with a pedal.

The exercises are designed to be played with a "strict four feel" (duple feel). I would strongly recommend you play System 1 and sing the eighth note subdivisions—instead of playing—them. Then go to the following set of variations and sing those and continue in this way. Singing the rhythms will pose a technical and coordination challenge, because your voice functions like another limb. Mastering the exercises in this fashion helps you internalize the rhythms and the general approach and will make playing the rhythms far easier.

Practice this system until you can play it with a good sound and feel, as well as a solid pulse. Basically, you need to be able to "play this in your sleep."

System 1

Once you can do this comfortably, continue to the next page. Here you continue to play the system with the corresponding limbs and play the variations (one-note through seven-note variations) in the left hand on the snare drum. Once you can execute these easily, you should also play the left-hand variations on other sound sources, as well as improvise by "breaking them up" onto varying sound sources in your set.

Finally, repeat each exercise numerous times, then continue on to the next without disrupting your groove. Read down the page playing each exercise two times each, four times each, and eighth times each.

On the subsequent six pages you will find the two-through-seven-note variations. Remember, after your basic execution is under control, the sound and the feel are your main concern.

Audio Note: In these examples the clave rhythm is played cross-sticked on the snare drum and the right hand plays the variations on the floor tom. The left foot is playing the downbeats of each bar on the hihat.

System 1

One-Note Variations

1.

2.

3.

4.

5.

6.

7.

8.

Audio Note: In these examples the clave rhythm is played cross-sticked on the snare drum and the right hand plays the variations on the floor tom. The left foot is playing the down-beats of each bar on the hihat.

System 1

Two-Note Variations

1.

2.

3.

4.

5.

6.

7.

8.

Audio Note: In these examples the clave rhythm is played cross-sticked on the snare drum and the right hand plays the variations on the floor tom. The left foot is playing the down-beats of each bar on the hihat.

System 1

Three-Note Variations

Audio Note: In these examples the clave rhythm is played cross-sticked on the snare drum and the right hand plays the variations on the floor tom. The left foot is playing the downbeats of each bar on the hihat.

System 1

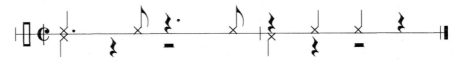

Four-Note Variations

1.

2.

3.

4.

5.

6.

7.

8.

Audio Note: In these examples the clave rhythm is played cross-sticked on the snare drum and the right hand plays the variations on the floor tom. The left foot is playing the down-beats of each bar on the hihat.

System 1

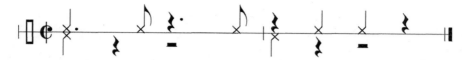

Five-Note Variations

1.

2.

3.

4.

5.

6.

7.

8.

Audio Note: In these examples the clave rhythm is played cross-sticked on the snare drum and the right hand plays the variations on the floor tom. The left foot is playing the downbeats of each bar on the hihat.

System 1

Six-Note Variations

1.

2.

3.

4.

5.

6.

7.

8.

Audio Note: In these examples the clave rhythm is played cross-sticked on the snare drum and the right hand plays the variations on the floor tom. The left foot is playing the downbeats of each bar on the hihat.

System 1

Seven-Note Variations

Audio Note: Example 30 is an improvisation using the clave and variations from the previous seven examples.

1.

2.

3.

4.

5.

6.

7.

8.

Creative Exercises
Melodic Permutations With Rumba Clave

The clave rhythm can also be treated as a melody. By revoicing this "melody" around the drum set we can create hundreds of new rhythmic patterns and musical possibilities.

If, for example, we take the clave and play this melody on two sound sources, such as hihat and cowbell (as in Example I), we have a new melody. The possibilities are limitless. In Example 2 we are using an L.P. Jamblock and emphasizing the bombo note by revoicing the "and" of beat 2 on the

large tom. Examples 3 and 4. demonstrate further melodic use of the toms.

Experiment with different voicings and orchestrations, then select one melody you like and go back to Part 1. Play through the exercises again, but now use your new melody in the system in place of the existing clave. This will introduce new technical challenges to overcome, but working in this fashion will give you much new technical ability and control and with it many new creative possibilities.

Audio Note: Example 30 is an improvisation using the clave melodic permutations from examples 1-4 above in one hand with variations played around the set with the other hand.

Part 3

Fundamental Concepts of the Cascara Rhythm

Changuito, Anga Diaz and "El Negro"

Gonzalo Rubalcaba, Roberto Vizcaino and Horacio

The Cascara

The cascara, which literally translated means "shell" is a very important ride pattern in Cuban music. It is a duple feel ride pattern that interacts in perfect harmony with the clave. In fact, it is the most common ride pattern in the son, guaracha, mambo and other similar dance styles. It is typically played by the timbalero (timbale player) on either the side of the timbales (the shell), on a cowbell or a cymbal cup.

It was derived from a strict eighth note subdivision using the following sticking:

R L R R L R L R R L R L R R L R

Try playing this rhythm first on the closed hihat. It is very important to create two different sound levels for the accented and unaccented notes. After you master the pattern above try doubling all the notes played by the left hand. The pattern then looks like this:

R L L R R L L R L L R R L L R R L L R

Try the following exercise first using both hands on the same sound source, i.e. closed hihat.

NOTE: This is not the way you would play the pattern in a musical setting. This is simply a technical exercise.

After you master this exercise, begin creating patterns by combining single and double strokes in the left hand.

These cascara concepts have been presented in the 3-2 clave position. However, you must practice all of these exercises in the 2-3 position as well. This is done by simply starting the pattern on the second measure.

Once you are comfortable with the exercise, try breaking up the left hand patterns around the kit.

One-Hand Cascara

The one hand cascara is derivative of the preceding rhythm but simply omits the left hand. Again, give special attention to the accents of the pattern.

Once you are comfortable with the cascara in one hand, add the clave rhythm in the other, then proceed to the following exercises and add the feet.

Cascara Rhythm in 3-2

Audio Note: Example 32 is the following example of the paila played with one hand. Audio Example 33 is the same pattern played with two hands. Follow the two-hand sticking given with the example.

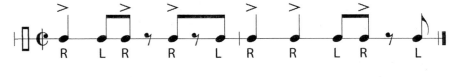

Cascara Rhythm in 2-3

Horacio with Walfredo Reyes Sr.

Part 4

Achieving Dexterity With the Cascara Rhythm

Raul Rekow, Giovanni Hidalgo, "Negro," and Karl Perazzo

Technical Exercises

Rhythmic Permutations With the Cascara

In this section we follow the identical approach of Part 2, where we addressed technical exercises with the clave. Here we apply the exact same system to gaining technical facility with the cascara.

Following is a series of permutation exercises designed to develop your independence, coordination, and sense of phrasing in this style of music. The hihat rhythm, played with the foot, is an important reference point, because it marks the downbeat of each measure and helps you to lock in the time.

The cascara rhythm is a very important rhythm in Afro-Cuban music, for it serves as the most basic comping (ride) pattern on timbales and drum set.

The cascara rhythm, played here with the right hand, can be played on any number of sound sources, such as a cowbell, woodblock (or L.P. Jamblock), auxiliary hihat, or the shell of the floor tom. Keep in mind the timbre you are trying to achieve. It should relate to the percussion instruments traditionally played in this style of music—especially if you wish to play with an authentic sound.

I also suggest that you practice Part 1 with your left hand playing cascara and your right hand playing the variations. Don't be afraid to break-up the rhythms around the drumset once you feel comfortable with the exercises.

You should also sing the variations as you play a system, as was started in Part 2. Keep in mind that you are working with a duple feel.

Finally, you can try going through these exercises with the 2-3 clave position. In other words, simply reverse the pattern and start on bar two.

Note: The notation and suggested orchestration of each of the following exercises is provided at each rhythmic pattern.

4

System 2

One-Note Variations

1.

Part 1

Audio Note: Example 35 is a seven-part example. It consists of Variation #2 from this page and Variation #2 on each page through page 44 played 2 times each back to back. Turn to the next page as the example plays to follow along. (Variation #2 on pages 38–44 played two times each.)

The cascara (system) is played on a cowbell with the left foot playing the downbeats on the hihat. The variations are played on the snare. As you develop facility with this approach, these patterns can be orchestrated in a variety of ways around your drum set.

2.

3.

4.

5.

6.

7.

8.

System 2

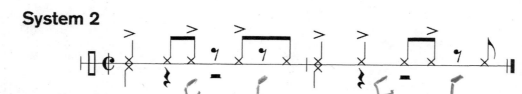

Two-Note Variations

1.

Part 2

**Audio Note:
Example 35 is a
seven-part
example. It
consists of
Variation #2
from page 38–44
played 2 times
each back to
back. Turn to the
next page as the
example plays to
follow along.
(Variation #2 on
pages 38–44
played two times
each.)**

2.

3.

4.

5.

6.

7.

8.

System 2

Three-Note Variations

1.

Part 3

**Audio Note:
Example 35 is a
seven-part
example. It
consists of
Variation #2
from page 38–44
played 2 times
each back to
back. Turn to the
next page as the
example plays to
follow along.
(Variation #2 on
pages 38–44
played two times
each.)**

2.

3.

4.

5.

6.

7.

8.

System 2

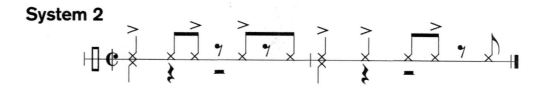

Four-Note Variations

1.

35

Part 4

**Audio Note:
Example 35 is a
seven-part
example. It
consists of
Variation #2
from page 38–44
played 2 times
each back to
back. Turn to the
next page as the
example plays to
follow along.
(Variation #2 on
pages 38–44
played two times
each.)**

2.

3.

4.

5.

6.

7.

8.

System 2

Five-Note Variations

1.

35

Part 5

Audio Note: Example 35 is a seven-part example. It consists of Variation #2 from page 38–44 played 2 times each back to back. Turn to the next page as the example plays to follow along. (Variation #2 on pages 38–44 played two times each.)

2.
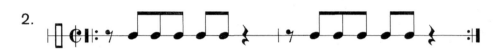

3.

4.

5.

6.

7.

8.

System 2

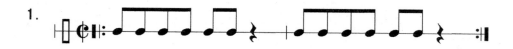

Six-Note Variations

1.

Part 6

**Audio Note:
Example 35 is a
seven-part
example. It
consists of
Variation #2
from page 38–44
played 2 times
each back to
back. Turn to the
next page as the
example plays to
follow along.
(Variation #2 on
pages 38–44
played two times
each.)**

2.

3.

4.

5.

6.

7.

8.

4

System 2

Seven-Note Variations

1.

Part 7

Audio Note:
Example 35 is a
seven-part
example. It
consists of
Variation #2
from page 38–44
played 2 times
each back to
back. Turn to the
next page as the
example plays to
follow along.
(Variation #2 on
pages 38–44
played two times
each.)

2.

3.

4.

5.

6.

7.

8.

Creative Exercises

Melodic Permutations With the Cascara Rhythm

Following are a series of rhythmic combinations written on a single line. You are to think of these rhythms as melodies and orchestrate them around your drumset-percussion setup.

You should start by simply playing the ostinato system and the "melody rhythms" on the snare. Once you are comfortable with the technical aspect you can continue with the following.

Your approach can be twofold. First, you can try playing repeating "melody rhythms" in order to create motifs. These can then become grooves you use in playing musical pieces and can even become the basis for a piece. Second, you can try to play from a purely improvisational perspective. Obviously your improvisations should consist of motifs and recurring themes, but here your challenge should be to see how far you can go with the orchestration of these patterns.

Your approach should start with the following ostinato systems:
  I. **Right hand plays rumba clave–left hand plays melody.**
  2. **Left hand plays rumba clave–right hand plays melody.**
  3. **Right hand plays cascara–left hand plays melody.**
  4. **Left hand plays cascara–right hand plays melody.**

The pattern you play with your feet is up to you. You should start with the downbeats in the hihat. Later in the book there are additional patterns to play with the feet.

Try to concentrate on phrasing and always strive for a good feel and dynamic balance.

Two-Note Melody Exercises

Audio Note: The cascara (system) is played on a cowbell with the left foot playing the downbeats on the hihat. The variations are played on the snare. As you develop facility with this approach, these patterns can be orchestrated in a variety of ways around your drum set.

1.

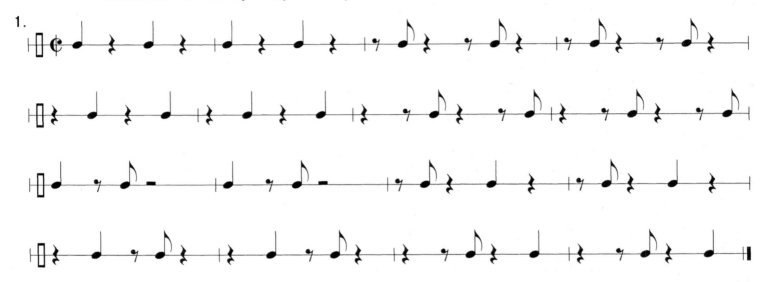

2.

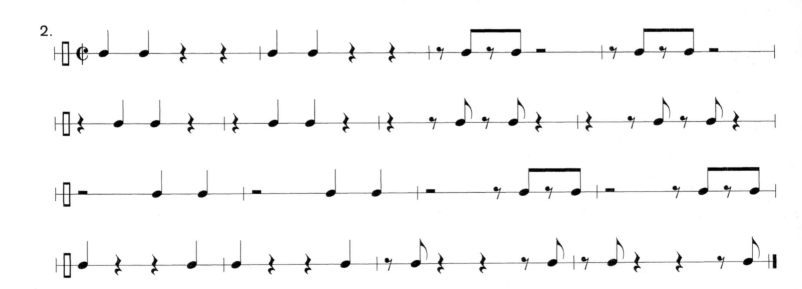

Two-Note Melody Exercises (continued)

3.

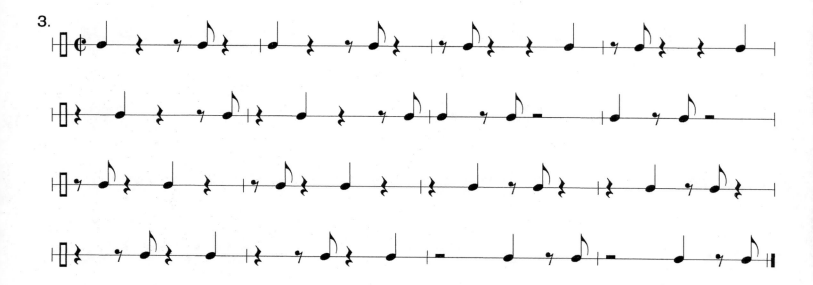

Three-Note Melody Exercises

1.
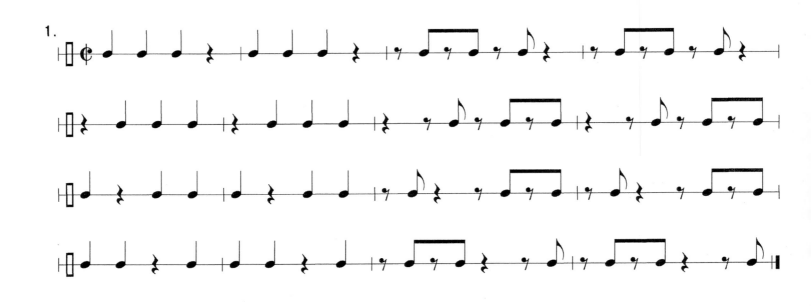

2.

Three-Note Melody Exercises (continued)

Audio Note: The cascara (system) is played on a cowbell with the left foot playing the downbeats on the hihat. The variations are played on the snare. As you develop facility with this approach, these patterns can be orchestrated in a variety of ways around your drum set.

3.

Audio Note: Example 38 is an improvisation orchestrating the rhythms from the previous example around the drum set.

4.

4

Three-Note Melody Exercises (continued)

5.

6.
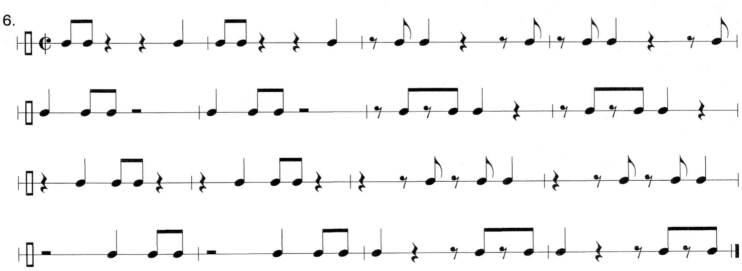

Four-Note Melody Exercises

1.
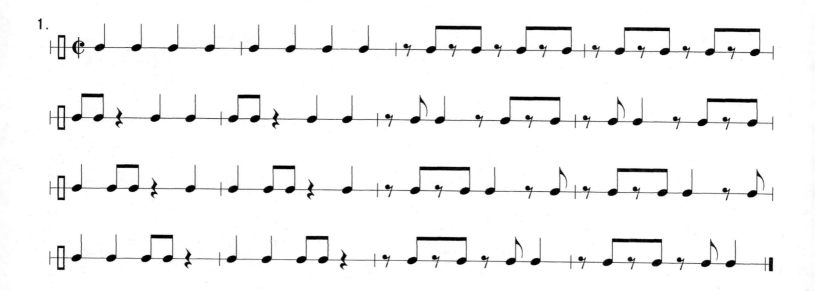

2.

4

Four-Note Melody Exercises (continued)

3.

4.

Four-Note Melody Exercises (continued)

5.

6.

Four-Note Melody Exercises (continued)

7.

8.

Four-Note Melody Exercises (continued)

9.

Applications In Improvisation

The final step in practicing the "melody rhythm" exercises is to improvise the rhythmic line as well as the orchestration (melody). Following are two examples of these exercises with the rhythmic line improvised, as would be done in an actual playing situation in which you are comping and improvising with these rhythms.

Take these improvised rhythmic lines and improvise melodies with them.

Audio Note: Example 39 is an improvisation using mixed rhythms, as in the following two examples, and orchestrating them around the drum set. The possibilities are endless as both the rhythms and the orchestrations are improvised.

Part 5

Fundamental Concepts of Afro-Cuban $\frac{6}{8}$

Horacio with timbalero Orestes Vilato

5

$\frac{6}{8}$ Clave

This section mirrors the approach taken in the last two sections—clave and cascara development respectively—and now applies them to Afro-Cuban $\frac{6}{8}$. This often-used term: "Afro-Cuban $\frac{6}{8}$ pattern" (or $\frac{6}{8}$ clave), is actually a generic term use to describe many different actual rhythms. Though many people use the term to describe a feel, they do not know the specific patterns in the particular styles. This section presents what is probably the most common of the patterns that are usually associated with the music called "Afro-Cuban $\frac{6}{8}$." The first two patterns notated below are different from each other, yet they are both often referred to as $\frac{6}{8}$ clave.

Pattern 2 is the pattern we will focus on in this section. It is often played on a hand-held cowbell at Bembes (religious gatherings), and other folkloric events featuring music with African roots. When practicing these technical exercises try to internalize this bell pattern as the clave. This bell pattern becomes the basic pulse to which all of the other rhythms conform.

Try playing the pattern on a cowbell or the bell of a ride cymbal. Then play the left-hand variations on one sound source, such as your snare drum. Once you feel comfortable with this, try "breaking up" the rhythms around the kit. Again, it is very important to listen to performances in this style of music to learn how to phrase with an authentic feel. Think of this approach as being the same as the approach you might take to study the jazz ride cymbal patterns of Elvin Jones or Tony Williams. After you overcome the technical hurdles, your phrasing, feel and steady tempo should be your main concerns.

1.

2.

5

Technical Exercises

Rhythmic Permutations With the Afro-Cuban $\frac{6}{8}$ Clave

The following exercises will help you gain control and dexterity with the Afro-Cuban 6/8 style. This section follows the same process as that of the clave and cascara sections. That is, we take a basic system and maintain it as an ostinato pattern in two limbs—in this case right hand and hihat—and play rhythmic permutations in a third limb (the left hand).

Remember that once you have the technical aspects under control, the feel and groove is the main concern. This is a triple-meter feel so you should practice singing an eighth-note triplet subdivision under all of these exercises.

The following pattern, System 3, will be your main system for this first set of exercises. Play the right hand on the cowbell, side of floor tom, cymbal bell, or closed auxiliary hihat, and play the hihat with the left foot. Remember that the hihat foot pattern playing the downbeats is establishing the basic pulse and the bell pattern is establishing the feel.

Once you have this system under control, proceed to the following patterns.

Keep in mind that the Afro-Cuban 6/8 clave and its related rhythms are triplet feels. It is a good practice to sing a triplet subdivision while practicing the following exercises. This will help you further "lock in" the rhythms.

System 3

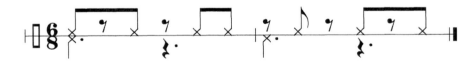

System 3

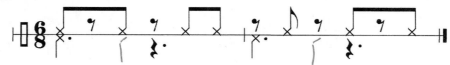

One-Note Variations

1.

2.

3.

4.

5.

6.

Fundamental Concepts of Afro-Cuban $\frac{6}{8}$

Audio Note: On the recording this system is played with one hand on a cowbell, the hihat playing the downbeats with the foot and the variations played on the snare with the other hand.

System 3

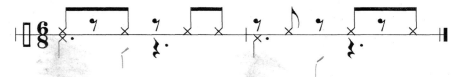

Two-Note Variations

1.

2.

3.

4.

5.

6.

Audio Note: On the recording this system is played with one hand on a cowbell, the hihat playing the downbeats with the foot and the variations played on the snare with the other hand.

System 3

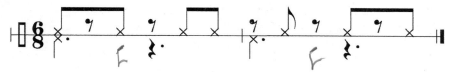

Three-Note Variations

1.

2.

3.

4.

5.

6.

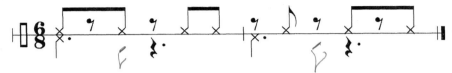

Audio Note: On the recording this system is played with one hand on a cowbell, the hihat playing the downbeats with the foot and the variations played on the snare with the other hand.

System 3

Four-Note Variations

1.

2.

3.

4.

5.

6.

Audio Note: On the recording this system is played with one hand on a cowbell, the hihat playing the downbeats with the foot and the variations played on the snare with the other hand.

System 3

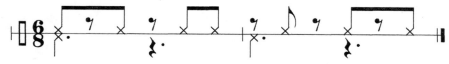

Five-Note Variations

1.

2.

3.

4.

5.

6.

Creative Exercises
Melodic Permutations with the Afro-Cuban $\frac{6}{8}$ Clave

Following are a series of rhythmic combinations written on a single line. You are to think of these rhythms as melodies and orchestrate them around your drumset-percussion setup.

You should start by simply playing the ostinato system and the "melody rhythms" on the snare. Once you are comfortable with the technical aspect you can continue with the following.

Your approach can be twofold. First, you can try playing repeating "melody rhythms" in order to create motifs. These can then become grooves you use in playing musical pieces and can even become the basis for a piece. Second, you can try to play from a purely improvisational perspective. Obviously your improvisations should consist of motifs and recurring themes, but here your challenge should be to see how far you can go with the orchestration of these patterns.

Your approach should start with the following ostinato systems:

1. **Right hand plays bell pattern–left hand plays melody.**

2. **Left hand plays bell pattern–right hand plays melody.**

3. **Right hand plays bell pattern–left hand plays melody.**

4. **Left hand plays bell pattern–right hand plays melody.**

The pattern you play with your feet is up to you. You should start with the downbeats in the hihat. Later in the book there are additional patterns to play with the feet.

The first and most basic foot pattern is to add the bass drum on the second note of the "three-side" of the clave.

Try to concentrate on phrasing and always strive for a good feel and dynamic balance.

Two-Note Melody Exercise

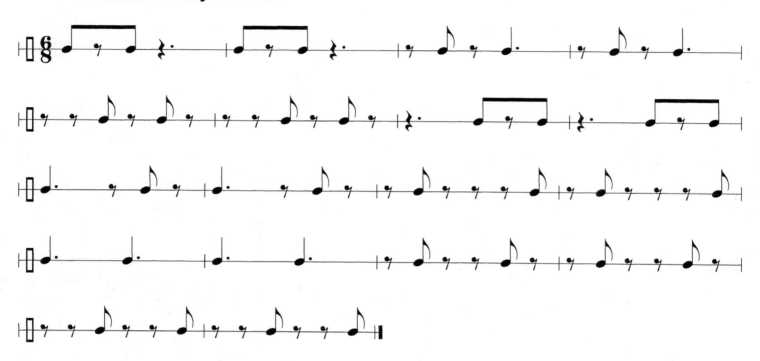

Three-Note Melody Exercise

Audio Note: On the recording this system (with the basic cowbell pattern) is played with one hand on the cowbell, the hihat playing the downbeats with the foot and the variations played on the snare with the other hand.

5

Four-Note Melody Exercise

Applications in Improvisation

The final step in practicing the "melody rhythm" exercises is to improvise the rhythmic line as well as the orchestration (melody). Following are two examples of these exercises with the rhythmic line improvised, as would be done in an actual playing situation in which you are comping and improvising with these rhythms.

Take these improvised rhythmic lines and improvise melodies with them.

Audio Note: Example 46 is an improvisation using mixed rhythms, as in the following two examples, and orchestrating them around the drum set. The possibilities are endless as both the rhythms and the orchestrations are improvised.

5

Variations for $\frac{6}{8}$ Rhythms

Following are a number of additional variations you can play with the rhythms presented in this section. The table shows you variations for the cowbell (ride pattern), bass drum, and hihat.

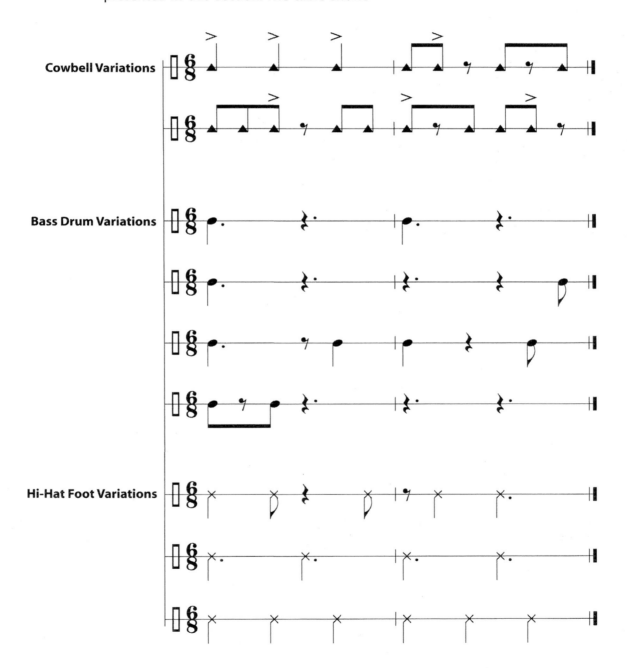

Part 6

Advanced Systems

Horacio with Michel Camilo

Technical Exercises
Preparatory Patterns and Combinations

Part 6 introduces more advanced systems comprised of three- and four-limb ostinato patterns with a variety of rhythmic combinations. The following preparatory exercises will give you the facility to begin working with the advanced systems. Begin by practicing each exercise slowly and carefully, then work them up to as many different tempos and dynamic levels as possible. Remember that the broader your dynamic and tempo range is, the more control you will have and many more musical possibilities will be available to you.

6

Hand Exercises Over Clave With Foot

These exercises will help you "line up" your alternating single and double strokes in the hands over the clave rhythm played with the hihat foot. Rhythmic accuracy is essential as is good sound, feel, and steady pulse.

1. Single Stroke Exercise

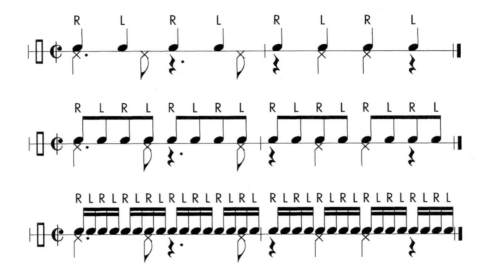

2. Double Stroke Exercise

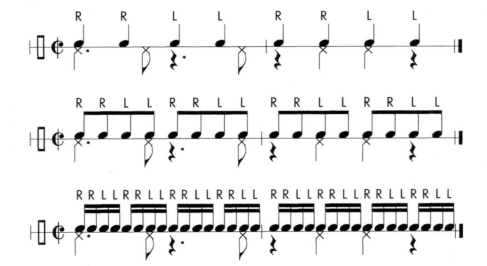

Cascara Independence Exercise

System

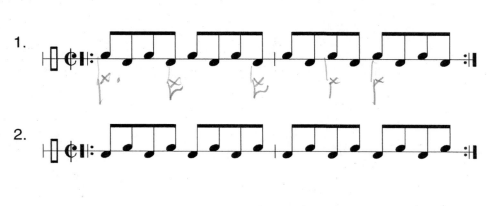

Bass Drum-Snare Drum/Right Foot-Left Hand Patterns

1.

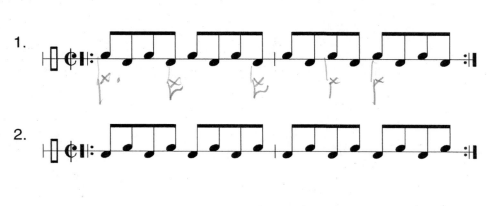

2.

3.

4.

5.

6.

6

Cascara Independence Exercise (continued)

Bass Drum Patterns

1.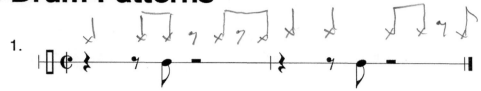

2.

3.

4.

5.

6.

7.

6

Hihat Patterns

1.

2.

3.

Victor Mendoza, Rod Morgenstein, Trilok Gurtu, Gregg Bissonette, Negro and Raul Rekow

Cascara Variations

Primary Pattern

1.

2.

3.

4.

5.

6.

7.

8.

System Exercises

Part 2 begins the advanced systems technical exercises. We'll start with a system comprised of the cascara pattern in the right hand, (played on any of the sound sources previously suggested), the rumba clave rhythm played on the hihat (or mounted L.P. Jamblock or cowbell) with the left foot, and the basic bass drum pattern (Pattern Number 1 from the Bass Drum Variations page.)

All of the systems are created by combining a cowbell or cascara pattern with the bass drum and a hihat patterns from the pages 77 and 78. Work with the systems written here and when you have mastered these you can develop your own combinations.

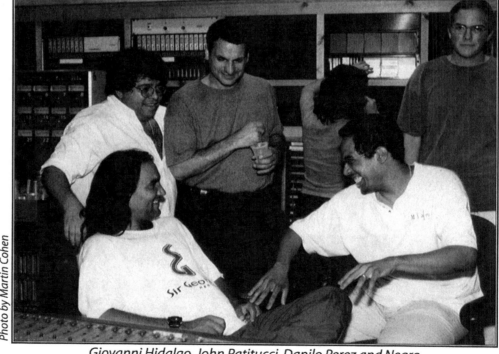

Photo by Martin Cohen

Giovanni Hidalgo, John Patitucci, Danilo Perez and Negro

System 1: Cascara and Clave With Bass Drum Pattern 1

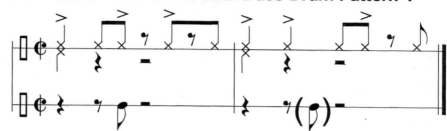

Audio Note: In the recorded example Horacio plays this cascara pattern but omits the bass drum in the second bar (the note in parenthesis) and plays the rumba clave with the left foot on a cowbell.

This is a more advanced version of this system. You should begin with the system as written here and then move to the more complex versions when you have the simple version mastered.

One-Note Left-Hand Variations

1.

2.

3.

4.

5.

6.

7.

8.

System Exercise 1

System 2: Cascara and Clave With Bass Drum Pattern 2

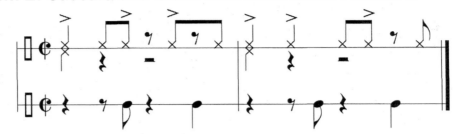

Audio Note: Shown here is System 2 with the Two-Note Left-Hand Variations.

On the recording Horacio uses System 1 to illustrate these two-note variations. You must practice these variations with all of the given systems.

Two-Note Left-Hand Variations

1.

2.

3.

4.

5.

6.

7.

8.

System Exercise 2

6

System 3: Cascara and Clave With Bass Drum Pattern 3

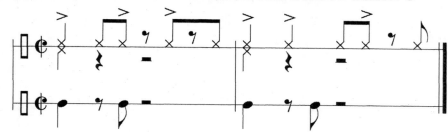

Audio Note: Shown here is System 3 with the Three-Note Left-Hand Variations.

On the recording Horacio uses System 1 to illustrate these three-note variations. You must practice these variations with all of the given systems.

Three-Note Left-Hand Variations

1.

2.

3.

4.

5.

6.

7.

8.

System Exercise 3

System 4: Cascara and Clave With Bass Drum Pattern 4

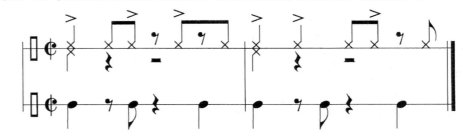

Audio Note: Shown here is System 4 with the Four-Note Left-Hand Variations.

On the recording Horacio uses System 1 to illustrate these four-note variations. You must practice these variations with all of the given systems.

Four-Note Left-Hand Variations

1.

2.

3.

4.

5.

6.

7.

8.

System Exercise 4

System 5: Cascara and Clave With Bass Drum Pattern 5

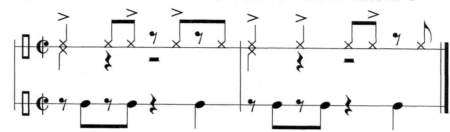

Audio Note: Shown here is System 5 with the Five-Note Left-Hand Variations.

On the recording Horacio uses System 1 to illustrate these five-note variations. You must practice these variations with all of the given systems.

Five-Note Left-Hand Variations

1.
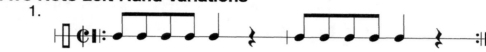

2.
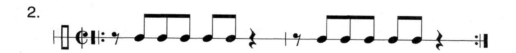

3.

4.

5.

6.

7.

8.

System Exercise 5

System 6: Mambo Bell and Clave With Bass Drum Pattern 1

Audio Note: Shown here is System 6 with the Six-Note Left-Hand Variations.

On the recording Horacio uses System 1 to illustrate these six-note variations. You must practice these variations with all of the given systems.

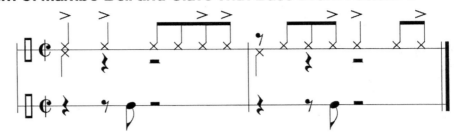

Six-Note Left-Hand Variations

1.

2.

3.

4.

5.

6.

7.

8.

System 7: Mambo Bell and Clave With Bass Drum Pattern 2

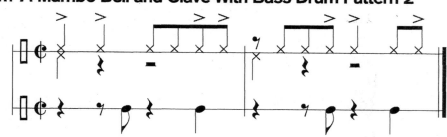

Audio Note: Shown here is System 7 with the Seven-Note Left-Hand Variations.

On the recording Horacio uses System 1 to illustrate these seven-note variations. You must practice these variations with all of the given systems.

Audio Note: Example 54 is an improvisation using System 1 with left-hand variations orchestrated around the drum set. Again, the possibilities in improvisation are endless.

First practice with simple rhythmic variations and orchestrations. As you become more proficient you will naturally begin playing more complex patterns.

Seven-Note Left-Hand Variations

1.

2.

3.

4.

5.

6.

7.

8.

System Exercise 7

6

System Exercise 8

The following pages contain the remaining systems —systems 10 through 15— shown with the one-note variations.

Practice each of the systems with all of the the left-hand variations— one through seven notes variations.

System 8: Mambo Bell and Clave With Bass Drum Pattern 3

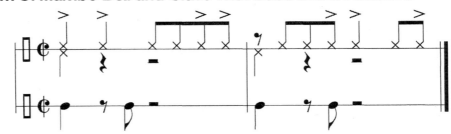

One-Note Left-Hand Variations

1.

2.

3.

4.

5.

6.

7.

8.

System 9: Mambo Bell and Clave With Bass Drum Pattern 4

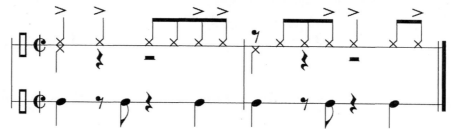

One-Note Left-Hand Variations

1.

2.

3.

4.

5.

6.

7.

8.

System Exercise 9

6

System 10: Mambo Bell and Clave With Bass Drum Pattern 5

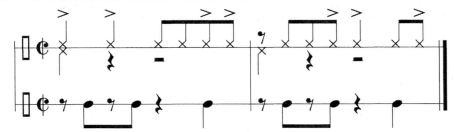

One-Note Left-Hand Variations

1.

2.

3.

4.

5.

6.

7.

8.

System 11: Bongo Bell and Clave With Bass Drum Pattern 1

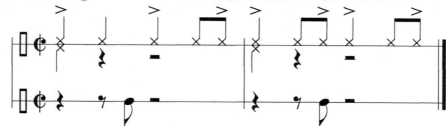

One-Note Left-Hand Variations

1.

2.

3.

4.

5.

6.

7.

8.

System 12: Bongo Bell and Clave With Bass Drum Pattern 2

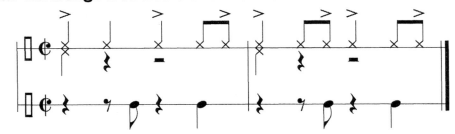

One-Note Left-Hand Variations

1.

2.

3.

4.

5.

6.

7.

8.

6

System 13: Bongo Bell and Clave With Bass Drum Pattern 3

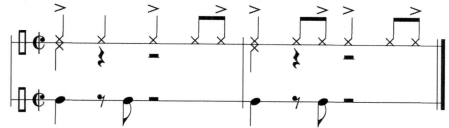

One-Note Left-Hand Variations

1.

2.

3.

4.

5.

6.

7.

8.

6

System Exercise 14

System 14: Bongo Bell and Clave With Bass Drum Pattern 4

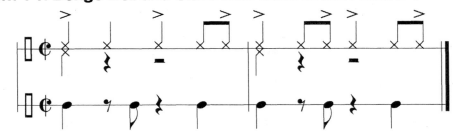

One-Note Left-Hand Variations

1.

2.

3.

4.

5.

6.

7.

8.

6

System 15: Bongo Bell and Clave With Bass Drum Pattern 5

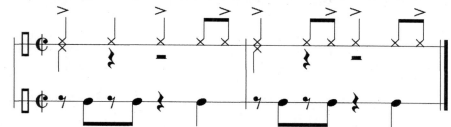

One-Note Left-Hand Variations

1.

2.

3.

4.

5.

6.

7.

8.

System Exercise 15

Creative Exercises

Your final practice sessions should focus on applying the techniques you've been learning in a musical way. You should focus on both a comping as well as soloistic approach, because both are necessary for musical performance.

Go back and play all 15 systems with melodic exercises listed in Section 8 Melodic Exercise Master Sets. Go back to Parts 1 and 2 if you need to refresh your memory for this approach.

Negro during a clinic performance at the Day of Percussion in Missoula, Montana

Part 7

Groove Transcriptions

Andy Gonzalez, Horacio and Giovanni Hidalgo

Introduction

This part presents transcriptions of grooves Horacio has developed and plays, as a matter of course, in his performances. These are not meant to be copied and played by you as the end. They are meant as a reference and a starting point for your to develop your own grooves.

You must be able to play these musical styles in order to perform in Afro-Cuban musical settings and in many settings where a "generic" approach to a particular Latin style is called for. In these situations you must play a "basic mambo" or a "basic songo" or whatever the musical situation calls for. But this should simply be a beginning for you to explore your creativity and these many rhythmic styles and develop your own versions of Afro-Cuban rhythms and also to integrate these rhythms with other musical styles.

Note:
The notation scheme for these transcriptions is as follows:
The patterns have been mostly notated on one-line staffs instead of five-line staffs for easier reading. In the case of cowbells and woodblocks, unique noteheads have been used for the various sound sources. *Each voice is notated at each example.*

7

$\frac{6}{8}$ Grooves for Drum Set

In the first groove Horacio uses a typical $\frac{6}{8}$ bell pattern but revoices the downbeat on the large tom to give more of a Bembe feel. Notice the hihat pattern simulates a shekeré pattern.

In the second groove the right hand is playing an Abacua pattern, which implies another (superimposed) meter. This is a very common characteristic of African music. He also plays the shekeré pattern with the hihat. Notice how the bass drum outlines the Abacua rhythm, implying a meter of three.

Afro-Cuban 6/8 Groove 1

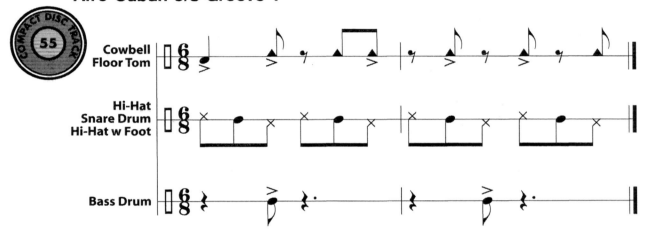

Afro-Cuban 6/8 Groove 2

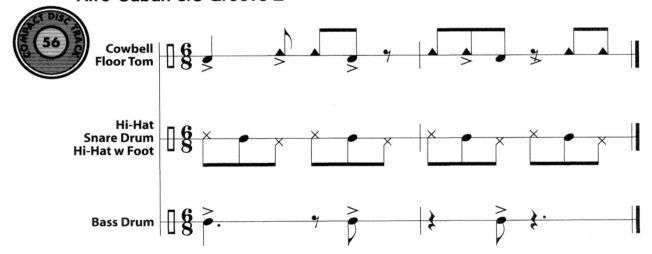

Audio Note: In this example Horacio plays the written pattern and then follows it with a short improvisation based on this rhythm.

Afro-Cuban ⁶⁄₈ Groove 3

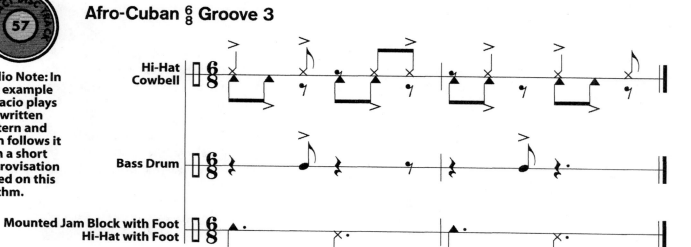

7

Guaguancó

Guaguancó is one of the most popular musical forms of the Cuban Rumba. The ensemble can be made up of percussionists, dancers and vocalists. In this highly complex form of music, the lead or solo drummer plays the quinto, skillfully mimicking the movements of the dancers while maintaining a conversation with the other two drummers—the salidor and the tres golpes. The middle drum, the Tres Golpes, and the lowest sounding drum, the Salidor, each play a specific melodic and rhythmic pattern that gives the Gauguancó its characteristic sound.

The drums are always accompanied by the clave and can include other various percussion instruments, such as the shekeré (a beaded gourd) and the guagua (a piece of bamboo mounted on a stand).

This example combines some of the basic Guaguancó patterns as applied to the drumset. It must be mentioned that the drumset is not played in traditional Rumba.

The tempo for Guaguancó is usually medium to medium-fast. The following pattern will also work on drumset for the Yambú, which is another form of Rumba that is slower in tempo.

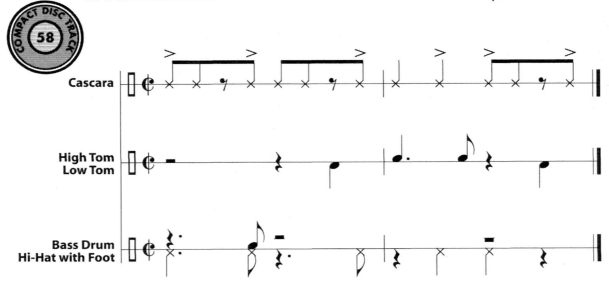

Mambo

The mambo is a popular Cuban dance rhythm that evolved from the Cuban Danzón style during the 1940s. The great composer and musician Israel Cachao Lopez is credited with further developing the mambo which became a staple for many of the Latin big bands in the United States during the 1950s.

The traditional percussion section calls for a congero, a timbalero, a bongocero and one of the orchestra musicians playing the clave (instrument).

Here is an example of a basic mambo pattern played on these traditional instruments. (Note the bongo bell pattern is played by the bongocero and the mambo bell pattern is played by the timbalero.)

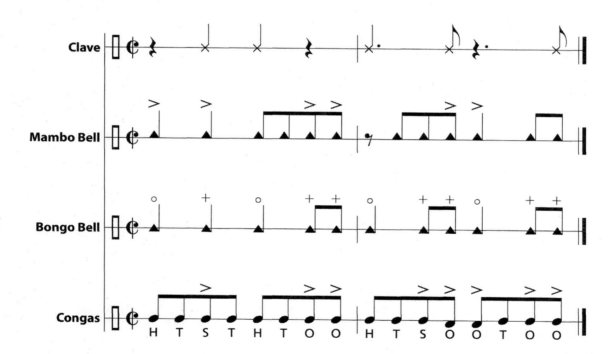

Mambo (continued)

The next example is a drumset application of the mambo, extracting rhythms from the traditional percussion instruments as played in the previous example. The mambo is generally played at medium to fast tempos.

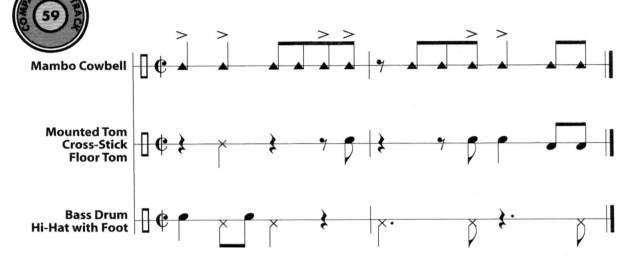

Conga and Comparsas

The conga is a carnival rhythm from Cuba. The rhythm (conga) is played in festivals and parades (comparsas). The music can be performed by singers, dancers and a band, complete with brass players and a full compliment of percussion instruments. Some of the more typical percussion instruments include various sizes of cowbells, congas (rebajadores and salidores), snare drums, bass drums, sartenes (mounted frying pans), and a host of other percussion instruments. Here is an example of a traditional conga followed by a drumset application.

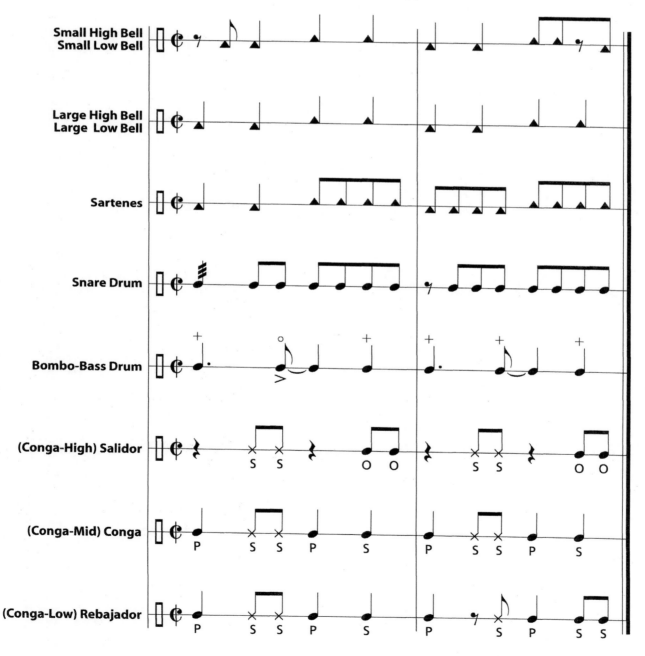

7

Conga (continued)

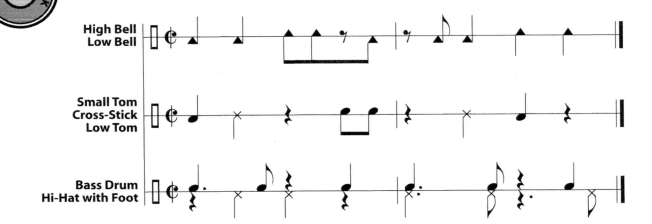

Cascara Groove

This is a good basic groove for many styles of Afro-Cuban music. It applies the cascara pattern, a bell pattern variation, a bass drum figure, and the 2-3 clave. This is a very versatile groove that can be applied to the drumset in many ways. Try revoicing some of the rhythms around the drumset. For example, substitute one of cascara notes for the snare drum, or try playing the bell pattern between two bells. The word cascara, literally translated, means shell, and, in Cuban music, cascara can either mean the actual rhythm itself, or it can indicate the percussionist should play on the shell (sides) of the drum (usually the timbales). In other words, one indication is for a rhythm, and the other is for a timbre.

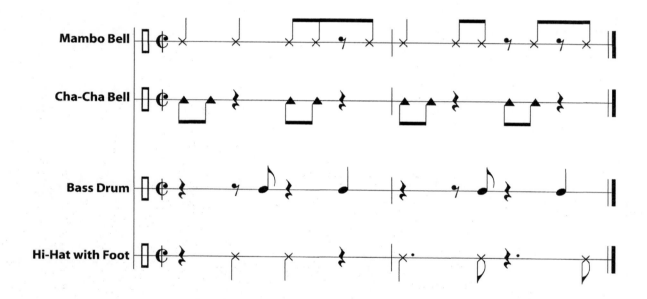

7

Macuta

The macuta is a unique rhythm that borrows elements from a variety of Cuban traditions, including traditional folkloric styles such as the rumbas as well as as more contemporary dance styles. The rhythm comes from the Bantu or Conga religion. It is usually played in the regions of Matanzas and Las Villas, where these religious sects are more popular. It has similarities to the Puerto-Rican Bomba rhythm, especially in the ride pattern. Horacio brings these elements together to form an interesting drumset groove.

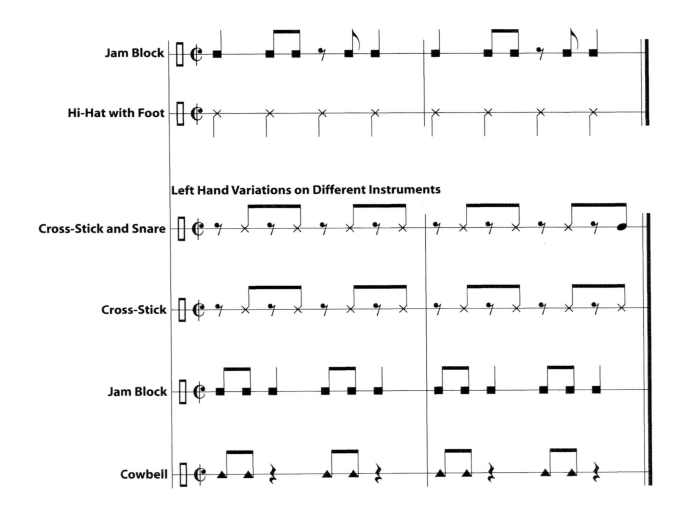

Cha Cha Cha

The Cha Cha Cha is a song and dance style that evolved from the Cuban Danzón. The name is taken from the sound of the dance steps. The tempo is usually played medium with a strong "four feel." Although less syncopated than most Afro-Cuban rhythms, the Cha Cha Cha's a unique groove that started a dance craze in the United States during the 1950s. The percussion instruments for this style typically include timbales, bongos, guiro and conga drums. Here are two examples of a drumset application.

61

Audio Note: Example 61 is a short improvisation based on the Cha-Cha groove.

62

Audio Note: On the recording Horacio improvises a cowbell and bass drum variation to this pattern.

1.

Cha Cha Bell Neck
Cha Cha Bell Mouth

Closed or Auxiliary Hi-Hat with Stick

Bass Drum

Hi-Hat or Jam Block with Foot

2.

Cha Cha Bell

Closed Aux. Hi-Hat
Snare Drum

Bass Drum

Hi-Hat with Foot

7

Merengue

The merengue has a wide variety of musical iterations. The most popular and well-known version is the one from the Dominican Republic, which is one of the most popular Latin dance forms throughout the world.

There are also variations of the merengue that emanate from Cuba and Haiti. Following is a drumset adaptation of a Cuban version. Notice that the pulse in the feet mark the downbeats—the same as the Dominican version.

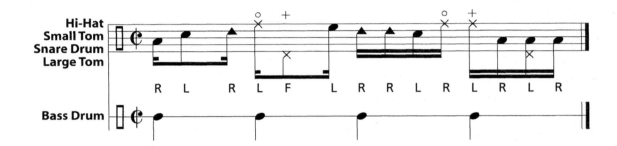

Songo

The songo has become one of the most popular rhythms played on the drumset—both in and out of Cuba. The key thing to remember, though, is that the Songo is not really a rhythm, but a way of playing. There are some fundamental rhythmic structures that are used to build beats, but the rest is up to the player and the particular musical setting.

Following is one of Horacio's adaptations for the drumset followed by an improvisation using his basic rhythm.

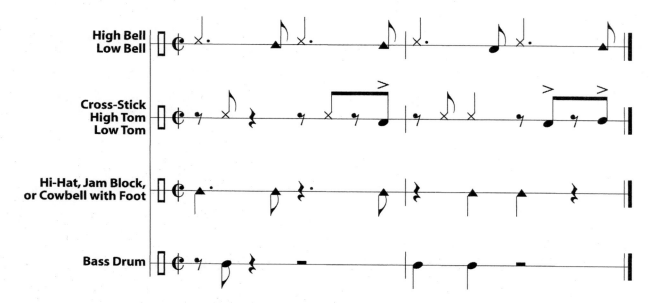

Audio Note: Example 63 is an improvisation based on the Songo style.

Audio Note: Example 64 is another improvisation based on the Songo style.

7

Mozambique

The mozambique is a rhythm that developed and flourished in the early 1960s in Cuba. It developed from a combination of the conga de comparsa and other Cuban carnival rhythms and elements of funk and related styles. It resulted in a very lively and syncopated style that contained many unique patterns but also left the players a lot of room for variations and improvisation.

The rhythm was popularized in Cuba by Pello El Afrokan and his ensembles and later made its way to New York where it was big influence in Latin dance styles as well as in jazz, funk and fusion styles. It has had many adaptations on the drumset, including typical and hybrid versions.

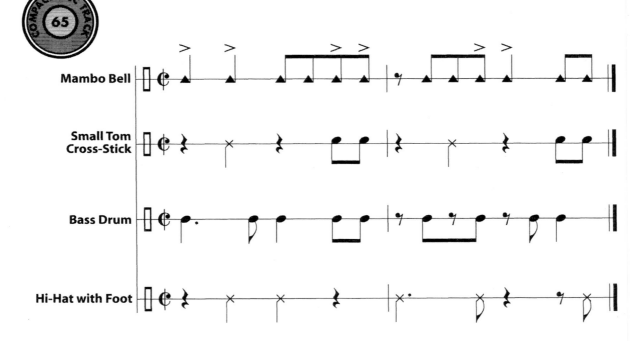

Recorded Grooves

The following are grooves Horacio plays on specific recordings. You can hear these grooves in their real setting by checking out the recording. Again, these grooves are here for you to learn and as a starting point to building your own variations. Do not just simply copy the grooves and leave it at that. You will never reach your maximum potential as a player if you do not develop your own voice and style.

Mambo de la Luna

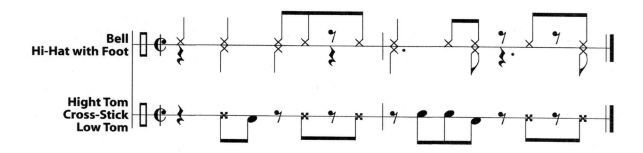

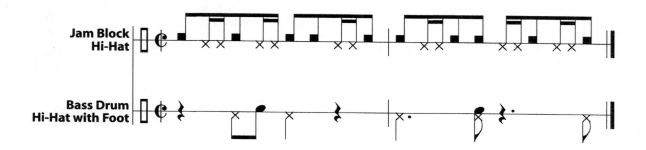

7

Sin Saber Porque

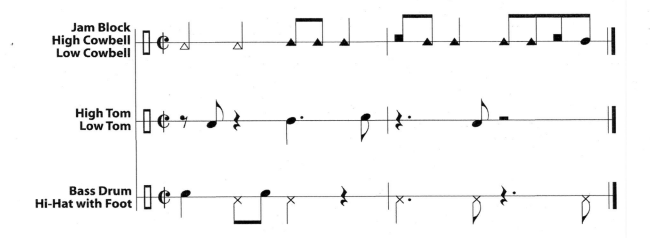

Part 8

Supplemental Materials

8

Left-Hand Variations: Master Sets

This section contains all of the left-hand variation master sets. They are listed here for convenience in reading through all of them in a practice session. You should practice all of these variations—the one-through seven-note sets—with all of the systems listed in Part 6. Practice each exercise slowly at first with the eventual goal of playing any variation with any system and moving from any variation to any other without any disruption to the feel. Practice all of these with a variety of tempos and dynamic ranges, as well as using different sound sources around your drum set.

Remember to stay focused on the feel and groove. This is the most important element in actually applying this material in musical situations.

One-Note Variations

1.

2.

3.

4.

5.

6.

7.

8.

8

Two-Note Variations

1.

2.

3.

4.

5.

6.

7.

8.

Two-Note Variations

Three-Note Variations

1.

2.

3.

4.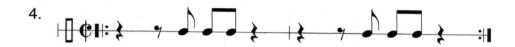

5.

6.

7.

8.

8

Four-Note Variations

1.

2.

3.

4.

5.

6.

7.

8.

Four-Note Variations

Five-Note Variations

1.

2.

3.

4.

5.

6.

7.

8.

Five-Note Variations

8

Six-Note Variations

1.
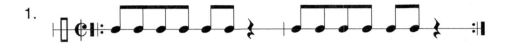

2.

3.

4.

5.

6.

7.

8.

Six-Note Variations

Seven-Note Variations

1.

2.

3.

4.

5.

6.

7.

8.

Seven-Note Variations

Melodic Exercises *(vertical side tab)*

Melodic Exercises: Master Sets

This section contains all the melodic exercise master sets. They are listed here for convenience in reading through all of them in a practice session. You should practice all of these variations with all of the systems listed in Part 6. Practice each exercise slowly at first, with the eventual goal of playing any variation with any system and moving from any variation to any other without any disruption to the feel. Practice all of these with a variety of tempos and dynamic ranges, as well as using different sound sources around your drum set.

Remember that the improvisation is not only in the rhythm but in the orchestration of the notes around the drum set. You create the "melodies" through your placement of the notes around the set. Try to establish themes with your placement of the notes by repeating things. This will help you develop your sense of phrasing.

Remember to stay focused on the feel and groove. This is the most important element in actually applying this material in musical situations.

Two-Note Melody Exercises

1.

2.

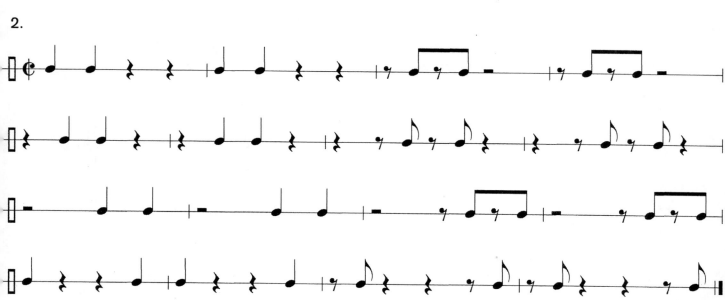

8

Two-Note Melody Exercises (continued)

3.

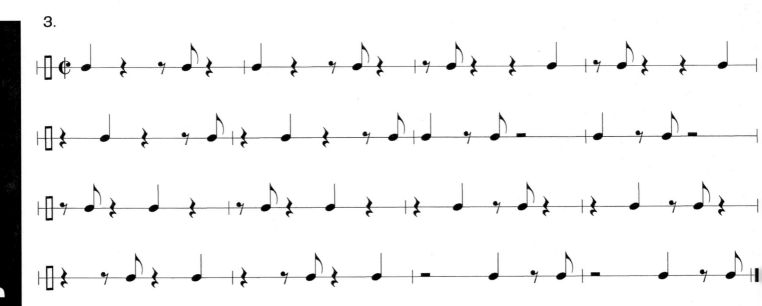

Three-Note Melody Exercises

1.

2.

Three-Note Melody Exercises

Three-Note Melody Exercises (continued)

3.

4.

Three-Note Melody Exercises

8

Three-Note Melody Exercises (continued)

5.

6.

Three-Note Melody Exercises

Four-Note Melody Exercises

Four-Note Melody Exercises (continued)

3.

4.

8

Four-Note Melody Exercises (continued)

5.

6.

Four-Note Melody Exercises (continued)

7.

8.

Four-Note Melody Exercises (continued)

9.

Selected Discography

With Gonzalo Rubalcaba
Grupo Proyecto
Live in Havana
Embele Iruke
Mi Gran Pasion
Giraldilla
Gonzalo Rubalcaba and Clark Terry in Finland
Gonzalo Rubalcaba and Dizzy Gillespie in Havana

With Carlos Averhoff
Solamente con Amor

With Cuban All Stars
Volumes I, II, and III

With Paquito D'Rivera
Forty Years of Cuban Jam Sessions, Volume I (featuring Cachao and Chocolate Armenteros)
A Night in Englewood

With Kip Hanrahan
Arabian Nights
Deep Rumba I and II (Hernandez, co-producer)

With Michel Camilo
Two Much (film soundtrack)
Thru My Eyes

With Tito Puente
Tito Puente and La India

With David Sanchez
Street Scenes

With Tropi Jazz All Stars
Tropi Jazz All Stars Volumes I & II

With Roy Hargrove's Crisoul
Habana (1997 Grammy Award for Latin Jazz)

With Steve Turre
Steve Turre

With Santana
Supernatural

With John Patitucci
Imprint

With Sergio George
Live With Sergio George

With Giovanni Hidalgo & Umberto Ramirez
Best Friends

With Joanne Brackeen
Pink Elephant Magic
Joe Henderson Tribute
Christmas Carols

With Arturo O'Farrill
Bloodlines

With Juan Carlos Formell
Songs From A Little Blue House

With Gabriella Anders
*New Recording-Title Unavailable

With Ilario Duran
Habana Nocturna

With Papo Vasquez
Pirates and Troubadors

With the All-Stars
Jammin' In The Bronx

With the United Nations Orchestra
Forty Years of Cuban Jam Sessions, Volume II (featuring Chucho Valdes)

With Ed Simon
El Dia que me Quieras

With Victor Mendoza
This is Why

With Dave Samuels
Tjaderize It!

With Santi Debriano
Suave
Circle Chant

With Juan Pablo Torres
Together Again

With Jack Bruce
Shadows In the Air

Paolo De Sabatino
Threeo

With Gary Burton
Gary Burton: For Hamp, Red, Bags, and Cal

With Ana Torroja
Pasajes de un Sueño

Chucho Valdez
Live In New York (CD and Video available)